It is a wet day in May. Jelly and Bean go to play on the hay in the little shed.

A hen is in the little shed. She is sitting on the hay. She gets up. Jelly and Bean see an egg on the hay.

The next day Jelly and Bean go into the little shed again. They see the hen on the hay. She gets up, and they see two eggs on the hay.

Then the hen sits on the eggs. She will not go away. She sits on them all day. She will not let Jelly and Bean play.

The next day Jelly and Bean go into the little shed again.
"You cannot play on the hay," says the hen.

"I am sitting on my eggs. I have to stay on them for twenty-one days. You must go away and play on the grass."

Jelly and Bean go away, but Kevin and Lotty go into the little shed to play. They see the hen sitting on the hay.

"You cannot play on the hay," says the hen. "I have to stay on my eggs for twenty-one days. You must go away and play on the grass."

Every day the cats and the dogs go into the little shed.
Every day they see the hen sitting on the hay.

Then on the last day ... tap ... tap ... tap. The two eggs crack, and the hen has two little chickens. Hurray ... hurray!

"ay"

May

hay

day

says

away

stay

play

hurray

High Frequency Words

and   to   on   the   in   a   she   go

all   dogs   I   am   for   see   day

away   play   cats   it   is   gets   up

they   my

little   one   an   next   again   must

has   then   will   not   have   them

last   two   but